Welcome  wonderful slang! If you've ever found yourself lost in tran while visiting Panama, fear not—this dictionary is your ultimate guide to cracking the code of local lingo. Whether you're trying to decode the cryptic language of a street vendor or impress your new friends with some spicy phrases, this book has got you covered. Get ready to laugh, learn, and maybe even raise a few eyebrows as you dive into the vibrant, quirky, and downright hilarious expressions that make Panamanian Spanish so unique. ¡Vamos a darle duro, parce!"

Where is your next travel?

SCAN THE QR

Get the Slang Dictionary Collection

Slang Dictionaries Availables:

- French
- Mexican
- German
- Italian
- Colombian
- Many More...

TABLE OF CONTENT

A *5*

B *8*

C *12*

D *16*

E *20*

F *24*

G *27*

H *30*

I *34*

J *38*

K *41*

L *43*

M *47*

N *50*

O *54*

P *58*

Q *62*

R *66*

S *69*

T *72*

U *74*

V *76*

W *77*

A

¡A la vida!
Expression of surprise.
Example: ¡A la vida, qué calor!
Translation: Wow, it's so hot!

A pata
On foot.
Example: Vamos a pata hasta la tienda.
Translation: Let's walk to the store.

A pelar
To leave quickly.
Example: ¡Vámonos, a pelar!
Translation: Let's go, quickly!

Abombado
Spoiled or rotten (food).
Example: Esta leche está abombada.
Translation: This milk is spoiled.

Acho
Expression of frustration.
Example: ¡Acho, no encuentro mis llaves!
Translation: Ugh, I can't find my keys!

Arrebatado
High on drugs or extremely excited.
Example: Ese man está arrebatado.
Translation: That guy is really high.

Ataja
To intercept or catch.
Example: Ataja ese balón.
Translation: Catch that ball.

Aplatanado
Used to describe someone who has adapted well to Panamanian culture.
Example: El gringo ya está aplatanado.
Translation: The foreigner is already well-adjusted to Panama.

Arranca
Go away or leave.
Example: ¡Arranca de aquí!
Translation: Get out of here!

Arrejuntarse
To live together without being married.
Example: Ellos se arrejuntaron hace años.
Translation: They've been living together for years.

Aguacero
Heavy rain.
Example: No salgas, está cayendo un aguacero.
Translation: Don't go out, it's pouring rain.

A la brava
Doing something recklessly.
Example: Se lanzó a la brava sin pensar.
Translation: He jumped in recklessly without thinking.

A la suerte
Leaving something to chance.
Example: Lo dejé a la suerte y funcionó.
Translation: I left it to chance, and it worked.

Atolondra'o
Confused or disoriented.
Example: Después de la fiesta, quedé atolondra'o.
Translation: After the party, I was disoriented.

Averigua'o
Nosy person.
Example: Ese man es bien averigua'o.
Translation: That guy is really nosy.

A lo loco
Without thinking.
Example: No hagas las cosas a lo loco.
Translation: Don't do things without thinking.

Apapachar
To pamper or cuddle.
Example: Me gusta apapachar a mi perrito.
Translation: I like to cuddle my dog.

A platilla'o
Flat broke.
Example: Estoy a platilla'o hasta la quincena.
Translation: I'm broke until payday.

B

Bacano
Cool, awesome.
Example: Esa fiesta estuvo bacana.
Translation: That party was awesome.

Bajareque
Light rain or drizzle.
Example: Solo está cayendo un bajareque.
Translation: It's just drizzling.

Bam
A fool.
Example: No seas bam, piensa bien antes de actuar.
Translation: Don't be a fool, think before you act.

Bofetón
A hard slap.
Example: Le dio un bofetón por hablar mal.
Translation: She slapped him for talking badly.

Bucha
A large amount of something.
Example: Tengo una bucha de trabajo.
Translation: I have a ton of work.

Bollo
Corn dough wrapped in a leaf.
Example: Me comí un bollo en el desayuno.
Translation: I ate a bollo for breakfast.

Bultrón
A big, clumsy person.
Example: Ese man es un bultrón, siempre está tropezando.
Translation: That guy is clumsy, always tripping.

Bulo
A lie or false rumor.
Example: Eso es puro bulo, no le creas.
Translation: That's just a lie, don't believe it.

Burundanga
Confusion or mess.
Example: Todo se convirtió en burundanga.
Translation: Everything turned into a mess.

Buruco
A young, mischievous child.
Example: Ese buruco no para de hacer travesuras.
Translation: That kid won't stop causing trouble.

Buzo
Alert or sharp.
Example: Tienes que estar buzo para evitar problemas.
Translation: You need to stay sharp to avoid trouble.

Buay
A tough person.
Example: Ese man es buay, no te metas con él.
Translation: That guy is tough, don't mess with him.

Bumpar
To bump into someone.
Example: Me bampé con ella en la calle.

Translation: I bumped into her on the street.

Bucha
Money.
Example: No tengo bucha para salir.
Translation: I don't have money to go out.

Brincón
Jumping around or hyperactive.
Example: Los niños están brincones hoy.
Translation: The kids are jumping around today.

Bembe
Party.
Example: Vamos para el bembe esta noche.
Translation: We're going to the party tonight.

Bembón
Big-lipped person.
Example: Ese man es bembón, tiene labios grandes.
Translation: That guy has big lips.

Batalla
Hard work.
Example: Esta semana ha sido una batalla.
Translation: This week has been hard work.

Bregando
Dealing with something.
Example: Estoy bregando con esta tarea.
Translation: I'm dealing with this assignment.

Baratillo
Cheap sale.
Example: Compré todo en el baratillo.
Translation: I bought everything at the cheap sale.

C

Cachetear
To slap.
Example: No lo cachetees por tonterías.
Translation: Don't slap him for silly reasons.

Cangrejo
Someone who complicates things.
Example: Deja de ser cangrejo y hazlo fácil.
Translation: Stop complicating things and make it simple.

Chantin
A small house or shack.
Example: Vivo en un chantin al final de la calle.
Translation: I live in a small shack at the end of the street.

Chévere
Cool, awesome.
Example: Esa película estuvo chévere.
Translation: That movie was cool.

Chilingo
Skinny person.
Example: Ese man es bien chilingo.
Translation: That guy is really skinny.

Chombo
A black person (informal, sometimes derogatory).
Example: El chombo de la tienda es buena gente.
Translation: The black guy at the store is nice.

Chon
Cheap person.
Example: No seas chon, paga lo tuyo.
Translation: Don't be cheap, pay your share.

Chucha
Expression of frustration or surprise.
Example: ¡Chucha, se me olvidó la llave!
Translation: Damn, I forgot the key!

Chuspa
Plastic bag.
Example: Dame una chuspa para llevar la comida.
Translation: Give me a plastic bag to take the food.

Chochera
Confusion or forgetfulness.
Example: Mi abuela ya tiene chochera.
Translation: My grandma is already forgetful.

Cocobolo
A type of tree, also used to describe something of low quality.
Example: Ese carro es un cocobolo.
Translation: That car is a piece of junk.

Cojelo suave
Take it easy.
Example: ¡Cojelo suave, no te apures!
Translation: Take it easy, don't rush!

Chivato
Snitch.

Example: No seas chivato, no cuentes lo que viste.
Translation: Don't be a snitch, don't tell what you saw.

Cremoso
Rich or affluent.
Example: Ese man es cremoso, vive en Costa del Este.
Translation: That guy is rich, he lives in Costa del Este.

Chocolito
Dark-skinned person.
Example: Ese chocolito juega fútbol muy bien.
Translation: That dark-skinned guy plays soccer very well.

Chucaro
Wild, untamed.
Example: Ese caballo es bien chucaro.
Translation: That horse is really wild.

Congo
A fool.
Example: No seas congo, eso es fácil de hacer.
Translation: Don't be a fool, that's easy to do.

Churuquita
Small or insignificant.
Example: Esa plata es churuquita comparada con lo que ganamos.
Translation: That money is nothing compared to what we earn.

Chiricano
Someone from the province of Chiriquí.
Example: El man es chiricano, se nota por su acento.

Translation: The guy is from Chiriquí, you can tell by his accent.

Clavo
Problem or difficulty.
Example: Estoy en un clavo con esta deuda.
Translation: I'm in trouble with this debt.

D

Dame un break
Give me a break.
Example: Dame un break, estoy ocupado.
Translation: Give me a break, I'm busy.

Dizque
Supposedly.
Example: Dizque va a llover, pero no creo.
Translation: Supposedly it's going to rain, but I don't think so.

Duro
Strong or tough.
Example: Ese man es bien duro, no se rinde fácil.
Translation: That guy is really tough, he doesn't give up easily.

Desparramar
To scatter or spread out.
Example: Desparramó la ropa por toda la casa.
Translation: He scattered the clothes all over the house.

Diablo rojo
Colorful, public bus.
Example: Me subí en el diablo rojo para ir al trabajo.
Translation: I took the colorful bus to work.

Dar en el clavo
To hit the nail on the head.
Example: Diste en el clavo con esa solución.
Translation: You nailed it with that solution.

Duro de matar
Someone who is resilient.
Example: Ese man es duro de matar, nunca se rinde.
Translation: That guy is tough to beat, he never gives up.

De pinga
Really cool or really bad (depending on context).
Example: Ese carro está de pinga.
Translation: That car is really cool.

Duro de roer
Difficult to deal with.
Example: Ese problema es duro de roer.
Translation: That problem is tough to solve.

Dar papaya
To make yourself an easy target.
Example: No des papaya en la calle.
Translation: Don't make yourself an easy target in the street.

Dale plomo
Go for it.
Example: ¡Dale plomo y termina el proyecto!
Translation: Go for it and finish the project!

Dale que dale
Keep at it.
Example: ¡Dale que dale hasta que termines!
Translation: Keep at it until you finish!

De a vaina
Barely or just in time.
Example: Llegué de a vaina para la reunión.
Translation: I barely made it to the meeting.

Diente de leche
Baby tooth.
Example: Mi hijo perdió su primer diente de leche.
Translation: My son lost his first baby tooth.

Desbarajuste
Mess or disorder.
Example: Esta casa está en desbarajuste total.
Translation: This house is in total disarray.

Despelote
Chaos or confusion.
Example: El tráfico es un despelote hoy.
Translation: Traffic is chaotic today.

Dizque fresco
Someone acting casually after doing something wrong.
Example: Hizo la broma y se quedó dizque fresco.
Translation: He made the joke and acted like nothing happened.

Desparpajo
Lack of shame.
Example: Habló con desparpajo frente a todos.
Translation: He spoke shamelessly in front of everyone.

Dime tú
Tell me.

Example: ¡Dime tú si esto no es injusto!
Translation: Tell me, isn't this unfair?

Desgonzado
Exhausted.
Example: Estoy desgonzado después de tanto trabajar.
Translation: I'm exhausted after working so much.

E

Echar un pie
To dance.
Example: Vamos a la fiesta a echar un pie.
Translation: Let's go to the party to dance.

Echa'o pa'lante
Someone who is determined and proactive.
Example: Ese man es bien echa'o pa'lante, siempre consigue lo que quiere.
Translation: That guy is very determined, he always gets what he wants.

Emberracarse
To get angry.
Example: No te emberraques por eso.
Translation: Don't get mad about that.

Enjaranarse
To get into debt.
Example: Me enjarané para comprar el carro.
Translation: I got into debt to buy the car.

Empalmarse
To stay up all night.
Example: Me empalmé trabajando.
Translation: I stayed up all night working.

Estar pela'o
To be broke.
Example: Estoy pela'o, no tengo ni un centavo.
Translation: I'm broke, I don't have a cent.

Echarle coco
To think hard about something.
Example: Échale coco antes de tomar una decisión.
Translation: Think hard before making a decision.

Encochinarse
To get dirty.
Example: Se encochinó jugando en el barro.
Translation: He got dirty playing in the mud.

Entra y sale
A frequent visitor.
Example: Ese man es un entra y sale en mi casa.
Translation: That guy is always coming and going from my house.

Estar comiendo cuento
To believe everything you hear.
Example: Deja de estar comiendo cuento, no todo es verdad.
Translation: Stop believing everything you hear, not everything is true.

Estar de goma
To be hungover.
Example: Estoy de goma después de la fiesta.
Translation: I'm hungover after the party.

Echar vaina
To tease or make fun.
Example: No le eches vaina a tu hermano.
Translation: Don't tease your brother.

Estar en las nubes
To be distracted or daydreaming.
Example: Hoy estás en las nubes, ¿qué te pasa?
Translation: Today you're distracted, what's wrong?

Estar a la viva
To be alert or aware.
Example: Siempre tienes que estar a la viva en la calle.
Translation: You always have to be alert on the street.

Echar un cuento
To tell a story.
Example: Voy a echarte un cuento bien interesante.
Translation: I'm going to tell you an interesting story.

Empatarse
To start a romantic relationship.
Example: Se empataron hace poco.
Translation: They started dating recently.

Estar en la cuerina
To be in a difficult situation.
Example: Estoy en la cuerina con este trabajo.
Translation: I'm in a difficult situation with this job.

Empinar el codo
To drink alcohol.
Example: Anoche empinamos el codo hasta tarde.
Translation: Last night, we drank until late.

Estar en salsa
To be in trouble.

Example: Si no haces la tarea, vas a estar en salsa.
Translation: If you don't do your homework, you'll be in trouble.

Echarle ganas
To put in effort.
Example: Échale ganas, tú puedes hacerlo.
Translation: Put in the effort, you can do it.

F

Fren
Friend.
Example: ¿Qué hay, fren?
Translation: What's up, friend?

Fajarse
To work hard.
Example: Me fajo todos los días en la oficina.
Translation: I work hard every day in the office.

Fulo
A person with light skin or blonde hair.
Example: Ese man es fulo, parece gringo.
Translation: That guy is blonde, he looks like a foreigner.

Fulo
Money.
Example: Dame un fulo para el taxi.
Translation: Give me some money for the taxi.

Fregar
To bother or annoy.
Example: Deja de fregar, que estoy ocupado.
Translation: Stop bothering me, I'm busy.

Fuego
Something or someone amazing.
Example: Ese carro está fuego.
Translation: That car is amazing.

Ficho

Someone who is sneaky or tricky.
Example: Ese man es un ficho, cuidado con él.
Translation: That guy is sneaky, be careful with him.

Fiar
To sell on credit.
Example: Me fían en la tienda de la esquina.
Translation: They let me buy on credit at the corner store.

Farándula
Gossip or entertainment news.
Example: Me encanta escuchar la farándula en la radio.
Translation: I love listening to gossip on the radio.

Fino
Elegant or sophisticated.
Example: Ella es bien fina, siempre viste a la moda.
Translation: She is very elegant, always dressed fashionably.

Fajón
A hard worker.
Example: Ese man es fajón, nunca se cansa.
Translation: That guy is a hard worker, he never gets tired.

Fuleco
A lie or false statement.
Example: Eso que dijiste es un fuleco.
Translation: What you said is a lie.

Fula
A fight or brawl.
Example: Se formó una fula en la discoteca.

Translation: A fight broke out in the nightclub.

Fuma'o
High on drugs.
Example: Ese man está fuma'o, mira cómo actúa.
Translation: That guy is high, look at how he's acting.

Fregar el plan
To ruin plans.
Example: No friegues el plan, todo estaba saliendo bien.
Translation: Don't ruin the plan; everything was going well.

Fuete
A whipping or harsh punishment.
Example: Le dieron fuete por llegar tarde.
Translation: They punished him for being late.

Fino
Cool, nice.
Example: ¡Qué fino está ese carro!
Translation: How cool is that car!

Frenético
Energetic or hyperactive.
Example: Estaba frenético en la fiesta.
Translation: He was hyperactive at the party.

Frito
Fried food, typically fish or meat.
Example: Me encanta comer frito en la playa.
Translation: I love eating fried food at the beach.

G

Gallo
Joke or prank.
Example: Eso fue un gallo, no te lo tomes en serio.
Translation: That was a joke, don't take it seriously.

Guial
Girl.
Example: Esa guial es bien bonita.
Translation: That girl is very pretty.

Goma
Hangover.
Example: Estoy con una goma horrible después de la fiesta.
Translation: I have a terrible hangover after the party.

Galleta
Slap.
Example: Le dio una galleta por faltarle el respeto.
Translation: She slapped him for being disrespectful.

Guaricha
A woman who likes to flirt.
Example: Esa guaricha está coqueteando con todos.
Translation: That woman is flirting with everyone.

Gamuza
A cloth used for cleaning.
Example: Pásame la gamuza para limpiar los vidrios.
Translation: Pass me the cloth to clean the windows.

Gallo pinto
A dish made with rice and beans.
Example: Me encanta comer gallo pinto en el desayuno.
Translation: I love eating rice and beans for breakfast.

Grillo
Someone who is uncultured or tacky.
Example: Ese man es un grillo, no tiene modales.
Translation: That guy is tacky, he has no manners.

Gorrear
To freeload or take advantage of others.
Example: Siempre quiere gorrear en las fiestas.
Translation: He always wants to freeload at parties.

Guaro
Alcohol, especially cheap liquor.
Example: Pasamos la noche tomando guaro.
Translation: We spent the night drinking cheap liquor.

Guiso
A shady deal or corruption.
Example: Se metió en un guiso con el negocio.
Translation: He got involved in a shady deal with the business.

Goloso
Greedy.
Example: Es bien goloso, siempre quiere más.
Translation: He's very greedy, always wants more.

Guabina
A coward.
Example: No seas guabina, enfréntalo.
Translation: Don't be a coward, face it.

Galleta de perro
Something of low quality.
Example: Ese televisor es una galleta de perro.
Translation: That TV is a piece of junk.

Gastar pólvora en zorrillo
To waste time or effort.
Example: Estás gastando pólvora en zorrillo con ese proyecto.
Translation: You're wasting your time with that project.

Gárgaras
To make excuses.
Example: No hagas gárgaras, asume tu responsabilidad.
Translation: Don't make excuses, take responsibility.

Guapo
Handsome or brave.
Example: Ese man es guapo, siempre ayuda a los demás.
Translation: That guy is brave, he always helps others.

H

Hacerse el loco
To pretend not to notice.
Example: Se hizo el loco cuando le pedí ayuda.
Translation: He pretended not to notice when I asked for help.

Hacer barra
To cheer or support.
Example: Vamos a hacerle barra al equipo en el partido.
Translation: Let's cheer for the team at the game.

Harto
Fed up or tired of something.
Example: Estoy harto de escuchar la misma canción.
Translation: I'm tired of hearing the same song.

Habladera
Constant talking.
Example: No soporto la habladera de esa gente.
Translation: I can't stand those people's constant talking.

Hacer la paz
To make peace or reconcile.
Example: Vamos a hacer la paz después de esa discusión.
Translation: Let's make peace after that argument.

Huevo
Something easy.
Example: Esa tarea es un huevo.
Translation: That task is easy.

Hombre de bien
A decent or honorable man.
Example: Mi papá siempre ha sido un hombre de bien.
Translation: My dad has always been an honorable man.

Hacer un papelón
To embarrass oneself.
Example: Hizo un papelón en la fiesta cuando se cayó.
Translation: He embarrassed himself at the party when he fell.

Hacerse bolas
To get confused.
Example: Me hice bolas con tantas instrucciones.
Translation: I got confused with so many instructions.

Hablachento
Talkative.
Example: Es muy hablachento, nunca se queda callado.
Translation: He's very talkative, never stays quiet.

Hojaldrería
Arrogance.
Example: Su hojaldrería no tiene límites.
Translation: His arrogance knows no bounds.

Hilar fino
To pay attention to detail.
Example: Hay que hilar fino en este proyecto.
Translation: We need to pay attention to detail in this project.

Huelepega
Glue sniffer, used to describe street kids addicted to inhalants.
Example: Lamentablemente, hay muchos huelepegas en la ciudad.
Translation: Unfortunately, there are many glue sniffers in the city.

Hablar paja
To talk nonsense.
Example: Deja de hablar paja y ponte a trabajar.
Translation: Stop talking nonsense and get to work.

Hecho leña
Worn out or exhausted.
Example: Después del partido, estaba hecho leña.
Translation: After the game, I was worn out.

Hacer caso
To pay attention or follow advice.
Example: Haz caso a lo que te digo.
Translation: Pay attention to what I'm telling you.

Hacerle el quite
To avoid or dodge something.
Example: Le hice el quite al tráfico tomando otra ruta.
Translation: I dodged the traffic by taking another route.

Habla claro
Speak clearly.
Example: Habla claro, no te entiendo.
Translation: Speak clearly, I don't understand you.

Hacerse el vivo
To act clever or smart.
Example: No te hagas el vivo, ya sé lo que hiciste.
Translation: Don't act smart, I know what you did.

Hasta la tambora
To be very drunk.
Example: Estaba hasta la tambora después de la fiesta.
Translation: He was very drunk after the party.

I

Irse en blanco
To miss an opportunity or fail.
Example: Fui al examen sin estudiar y me fui en blanco.
Translation: I went to the exam without studying and failed.

Intrépido
Someone daring or bold.
Example: Ese man es bien intrépido, nunca tiene miedo.
Translation: That guy is very daring, he's never afraid.

Irse en banda
To lose control or go overboard.
Example: Se fue en banda con los tragos anoche.
Translation: He went overboard with the drinks last night.

Irarse
To get angry or upset.
Example: No te iras, solo es un chiste.
Translation: Don't get upset, it's just a joke.

Involucrado
Being involved in something, often with a negative connotation.
Example: Está involucrado en un problema legal.
Translation: He's involved in a legal problem.

Ir a la brava
To go into something without preparation.
Example: No puedes ir a la brava, necesitas planear mejor.

Translation: You can't go in unprepared, you need to plan better.

Ir de rumba
To go partying.
Example: Vamos a ir de rumba este fin de semana.
Translation: We're going to party this weekend.

Ir a la patada
To do something poorly or without care.
Example: Hicieron el trabajo a la patada, no quedó bien.
Translation: They did the job poorly, it didn't turn out well.

Imbancable
Someone or something unbearable.
Example: Ese man es imbancable, nadie lo soporta.
Translation: That guy is unbearable, no one can stand him.

Ira
Extreme anger or rage.
Example: Sentí mucha ira cuando me mintieron.
Translation: I felt a lot of rage when they lied to me.

Intrigar
To gossip or spread rumors.
Example: Siempre anda intrigando sobre los demás.
Translation: He's always gossiping about others.

Irse al suave
To take it easy.
Example: Vamos a irnos al suave, no hay prisa.
Translation: Let's take it easy, there's no rush.

Ir a la brava
To rush into something.
Example: No vayas a la brava, piénsalo bien.
Translation: Don't rush into it, think it over.

Irse de capirote
To go crazy or lose control.
Example: Se fue de capirote cuando se enteró de la noticia.
Translation: He went crazy when he heard the news.

Irse de boca
To speak too soon or say something inappropriate.
Example: Te fuiste de boca, no debiste decir eso.
Translation: You spoke too soon, you shouldn't have said that.

Interino
Temporary or acting in a position.
Example: Es el jefe interino hasta que nombren a alguien fijo.
Translation: He's the acting boss until they appoint someone permanent.

Irse a pique
To collapse or fail.
Example: El negocio se fue a pique durante la pandemia.
Translation: The business collapsed during the pandemic.

Ir de boca en boca
To spread by word of mouth.
Example: Esa noticia va de boca en boca por todo el barrio.

Translation: That news is spreading by word of mouth throughout the neighborhood.

Ir a la segura
To play it safe.
Example: Mejor vamos a la segura y no arriesgamos nada.
Translation: Better to play it safe and not risk anything.

Intrincado
Complicated or difficult to understand.
Example: Ese asunto es bien intrincado, no sé cómo resolverlo.
Translation: That matter is very complicated, I don't know how to solve it.

J

Jalar
To pull or to leave.
Example: Vamos a jalar de aquí, está aburrido.
Translation: Let's leave here, it's boring.

Juega vivo
Stay alert, be smart.
Example: En esta ciudad tienes que jugar vivo.
Translation: In this city, you have to stay alert.

Joda
Annoyance or trouble.
Example: No me metas en esa joda.
Translation: Don't involve me in that trouble.

Jurado
Sworn to secrecy.
Example: Estoy jurado, no diré nada.
Translation: I'm sworn to secrecy, I won't say anything.

Juma
Drunk.
Example: Se agarró una juma terrible anoche.
Translation: He got terribly drunk last night.

Jorobar
To bother or annoy.
Example: Deja de jorobar, estoy ocupado.
Translation: Stop bothering me, I'm busy.

Jugar a la casita

To play house, often in a romantic context.
Example: Ellos están jugando a la casita, pero no es serio.
Translation: They're playing house, but it's not serious.

Jopar
To push or shove.
Example: No me jopes, que me voy a caer.
Translation: Don't shove me, I'm going to fall.

Jalón
A ride or lift.
Example: ¿Me das un jalón hasta la esquina?
Translation: Can you give me a ride to the corner?

Jugar con candela
To play with fire, to take risks.
Example: Estás jugando con candela al hacer eso.
Translation: You're playing with fire by doing that.

Jartarse
To eat a lot, to be full.
Example: Me jarté de comida en la fiesta.
Translation: I ate a lot at the party.

Jefecito
A playful way to refer to your boss.
Example: ¿Qué dice el jefecito hoy?
Translation: What does the boss say today?

Joropo
A mess or chaos.
Example: Esto es un joropo, todo está desorganizado.
Translation: This is a mess, everything is disorganized.

Jugar de vivo
To act smarter or superior.
Example: No juegues de vivo, que aquí todos sabemos cómo es la cosa.
Translation: Don't act smarter, we all know how things work here.

Julepe
A scare or shock.
Example: Me dio un julepe cuando escuché ese ruido.
Translation: I got a scare when I heard that noise.

Jaleo
Commotion or fuss.
Example: ¿Qué es ese jaleo en la calle?
Translation: What's that commotion in the street?

Jocote
A type of fruit, also used to refer to someone stubborn.
Example: Ese man es un jocote, no cambia de opinión.
Translation: That guy is stubborn, he doesn't change his mind.

Jeta de chopa
A derogatory term for someone unattractive.
Example: Ese man tiene jeta de chopa, pobrecito.
Translation: That guy is really unattractive, poor thing.

K

Kanky
A messy or chaotic situation.
Example: Esa fiesta fue un kanky total.
Translation: That party was a total mess.

Kikí
Party or celebration.
Example: El sábado vamos a un kikí en la playa.
Translation: On Saturday, we're going to a party at the beach.

Kilo
Money, often a large amount.
Example: Eso te va a costar un kilo.
Translation: That's going to cost you a lot of money.

Kote
A nickname for a tough or strong person.
Example: Ese man es un kote, siempre está listo para pelear.
Translation: That guy is tough, always ready to fight.

Kakú
A colloquial term for a friend or buddy.
Example: Oye, kakú, ¿qué vas a hacer hoy?
Translation: Hey, buddy, what are you doing today?

Kao
Tired or worn out.
Example: Estoy kao después de tanto trabajo.
Translation: I'm worn out after so much work.

Kiwi
A playful nickname for someone.
Example: Oye, Kiwi, ven acá.
Translation: Hey, Kiwi, come here.

Kurtu
Short or curt in response.
Example: Su respuesta fue kurtu, no dijo mucho.
Translation: His response was curt, he didn't say much.

Kharma
The concept of karma, but used colloquially.
Example: Todo eso es kharma, cuidado con lo que haces.
Translation: That's all karma, be careful with what you do.

Kafú
A nickname for someone clever or quick-witted.
Example: Ese man es un kafú, siempre tiene una respuesta rápida.
Translation: That guy is clever, always has a quick response.

L

Lambón
Someone who sucks up or is overly flattering.
Example: Ese man es un lambón, siempre buscando quedar bien.
Translation: That guy is a suck-up, always trying to look good.

Leca
Light or not heavy.
Example: Esta caja está leca, no pesa nada.
Translation: This box is light, it weighs nothing.

Llenarse la boca
To boast or brag.
Example: Se llena la boca hablando de sus logros.
Translation: He boasts about his achievements.

Loco como una cabra
Crazy.
Example: Ese man está loco como una cabra, no le hagas caso.
Translation: That guy is crazy, don't pay attention to him.

Lenteja
Slow or sluggish.
Example: No seas lenteja, apúrate.
Translation: Don't be slow, hurry up.

Lambetón
Someone greedy or overly eager for something.
Example: Es un lambetón con la comida.

Translation: He's greedy with food.

Ladrón en pausa
Someone lazy, doing nothing.
Example: Ese man parece un ladrón en pausa, no hace nada.
Translation: That guy seems like a lazy bum, he does nothing.

Lindo y querido
Someone charming or lovable.
Example: Ese niño es lindo y querido por todos.
Translation: That kid is charming and loved by everyone.

Lárgate
Get out or leave.
Example: ¡Lárgate de aquí, no te quiero ver!
Translation: Get out of here, I don't want to see you!

Lío
Trouble or problem.
Example: Nos metimos en un lío con la policía.
Translation: We got into trouble with the police.

Lambear
To lick or be greedy.
Example: No lambes todo el helado, comparte un poco.
Translation: Don't lick all the ice cream, share some.

Lagartija
Someone who is sneaky or untrustworthy.
Example: Ese man es una lagartija, no le confíes nada.

Translation: That guy is sneaky, don't trust him with anything.

Lechón
Pig or glutton.
Example: Comió como un lechón en la cena.
Translation: He ate like a pig at dinner.

Loco de patio
Someone who acts strangely.
Example: Está como un loco de patio, hablando solo.
Translation: He's acting strange, talking to himself.

Ligar
To flirt or hook up.
Example: Se la pasó ligando toda la noche en la fiesta.
Translation: He spent the whole night flirting at the party.

Lunático
Someone eccentric or unpredictable.
Example: Ese man es un lunático, nunca sabes lo que va a hacer.
Translation: That guy is unpredictable, you never know what he'll do.

Llamar la atención
To attract attention.
Example: Siempre quiere llamar la atención con su ropa llamativa.
Translation: She always wants to attract attention with her flashy clothes.

Llorón

Crybaby or someone who complains a lot.
Example: No seas llorón, acepta la derrota.
Translation: Don't be a crybaby, accept the defeat.

Lleno hasta el tope
Completely full.
Example: El bus está lleno hasta el tope, no cabe nadie más.
Translation: The bus is completely full, no one else can fit.

Llevarse bien
To get along.
Example: Nos llevamos bien desde que nos conocimos.
Translation: We've gotten along since we met.

M

Manito
Little brother or close friend.
Example: ¿Qué pasa, manito? ¿Todo bien?
Translation: What's up, little bro? All good?

Mandón
Someone bossy or authoritative.
Example: Mi jefe es un mandón, siempre quiere que todo se haga a su manera.
Translation: My boss is bossy; he always wants everything done his way.

Mamey
Something easy or simple.
Example: Ese examen fue un mamey, lo pasé sin problemas.
Translation: That exam was easy; I passed it without any problems.

Mala leche
Bad luck or someone mean-spirited.
Example: Ese tipo siempre tiene mala leche, no le des bola.
Translation: That guy always has bad luck, don't pay attention to him.

Manga por hombro
Something disorganized or messy.
Example: Tu cuarto está manga por hombro, arréglalo.
Translation: Your room is a mess, tidy it up.

Matar tigre

To take on a side job for extra money.
Example: Estoy matando tigres los fines de semana para ganar un poco más.
Translation: I'm taking side jobs on the weekends to earn a bit more.

Moche
A cut or a share, especially money.
Example: El jefe se quedó con un buen moche del negocio.
Translation: The boss kept a good share of the deal.

Monda
Nothing important or worthless.
Example: Eso que dijiste no vale ni monda.
Translation: What you said isn't worth anything.

Morado
To be completely drunk.
Example: Estaba tan morado que ni podía caminar.
Translation: He was so drunk that he couldn't even walk.

Mosquearse
To get suspicious or irritated.
Example: Se mosqueó cuando le pregunté por su ex.
Translation: He got irritated when I asked about his ex.

Mulero
Someone who works hard, like a mule.
Example: Ese man es un mulero, nunca para de trabajar.
Translation: That guy is a hard worker, he never stops working.

Muerto de hambre

Someone desperate or greedy.
Example: No seas muerto de hambre, comparte un poco.
Translation: Don't be greedy, share a bit.

Mucha tela que cortar
A lot of work or things left to do.
Example: Todavía hay mucha tela que cortar en este proyecto.
Translation: There's still a lot of work left to do on this project.

Mete la pata
To mess up or make a mistake.
Example: Metió la pata en la reunión y ahora todos están molestos.
Translation: He messed up in the meeting, and now everyone's upset.

Manda fuego
To act recklessly or dangerously.
Example: Ese man manda fuego cuando maneja.
Translation: That guy drives recklessly.

Mente de pollo
Someone who is scatterbrained or forgetful.
Example: No confíes en él, tiene mente de pollo.
Translation: Don't trust him; he's scatterbrained.

N

Ñampe
To steal or take something without permission.
Example: Alguien ñampó mi comida de la nevera.
Translation: Someone stole my food from the fridge.

Nica
A short form of Nicaraguan, also used to describe something of low quality.
Example: Ese televisor es bien nica, no dura nada.
Translation: That TV is low quality, it doesn't last.

Ñeque
Strength, determination, or resilience.
Example: Hay que tener ñeque para terminar este trabajo.
Translation: You need determination to finish this job.

Ñangara
Someone lazy or laid-back.
Example: Deja de ser ñangara y ponte a trabajar.
Translation: Stop being lazy and start working.

Nítido
Clear, sharp, or perfect.
Example: Esa foto quedó nítida, parece profesional.
Translation: That picture is sharp; it looks professional.

No da pie con bola
To be unable to do something right.
Example: Hoy no doy pie con bola, todo me sale mal.
Translation: Today I can't do anything right, everything's going wrong.

Ñata
Someone with a flat or small nose.
Example: Esa chica tiene una ñata bien bonita.
Translation: That girl has a cute small nose.

Ñañeco
A small or weak person.
Example: No seas ñañeco, atrévete a hacerlo.
Translation: Don't be weak, dare to do it.

Nervioso como un pavo en Navidad
Very nervous.
Example: Estoy nervioso como un pavo en Navidad antes de la entrevista.
Translation: I'm as nervous as a turkey at Christmas before the interview.

Ñongos
Old or worn-out shoes.
Example: Esos ñongos ya no sirven, cómprate unos nuevos.
Translation: Those old shoes aren't good anymore, buy some new ones.

Ñeñeque
Another term for someone with strength or grit.
Example: Ese man tiene ñeñeque, no se rinde fácilmente.
Translation: That guy has grit; he doesn't give up easily.

Nena
A term of endearment for a young woman or girlfriend.
Example: ¿Cómo estás, nena?

Translation: How are you, girl?

Neto
Something genuine or authentic.
Example: Ese tipo es neto, no finge nada.
Translation: That guy is genuine; he doesn't pretend anything.

Ñoco
A person missing a finger or limb.
Example: Ese man es ñoco, pero aún así juega fútbol.
Translation: That guy is missing a finger, but he still plays soccer.

Nada del otro mundo
Nothing special.
Example: Esa película no es nada del otro mundo.
Translation: That movie isn't anything special.

Ñáñara
Goosebumps or chills.
Example: Me dio ñáñara cuando vi esa película de terror.
Translation: I got goosebumps when I watched that horror movie.

Ñame
Someone foolish or naive.
Example: No seas ñame, piensa antes de hablar.
Translation: Don't be foolish, think before you speak.

No te vayas a voltear
Don't change your mind or betray.
Example: No te vayas a voltear, confío en ti.

Translation: Don't change your mind; I trust you.

Ñeñe
A whiny or annoying person.
Example: No seas ñeñe, todo el tiempo te quejas.
Translation: Don't be annoying; you complain all the time.

No seas pendejo
Don't be stupid or gullible.
Example: No seas pendejo, te están tomando el pelo.
Translation: Don't be stupid; they're pulling your leg.

O

Ojo al cristo
Be careful or pay attention.
Example: Ojo al cristo, que ese negocio no pinta bien.
Translation: Be careful, that deal doesn't look good.

Oír campanas y no saber dónde
To hear something and not fully understand it.
Example: Estás oyendo campanas y no sabes dónde, infórmate bien.
Translation: You're hearing something and don't understand it, get properly informed.

Oído
Someone who listens well or a term for a close friend.
Example: Siempre puedes contar con mi oído.
Translation: You can always count on me to listen.

Ojo de halcón
A sharp observer or someone with keen vision.
Example: Necesitamos tu ojo de halcón para encontrar ese objeto perdido.
Translation: We need your keen eye to find that lost item.

Ojo al dato
Pay close attention to detail.
Example: Ojo al dato, que los detalles son importantes.
Translation: Pay close attention to detail, as the specifics are important.

Oído de oro
Someone with a great ear for music or sound.

Example: Ella tiene un oído de oro para la música clásica.
Translation: She has a great ear for classical music.

Oír cáscaras
To hear gossip or unconfirmed news.
Example: Solo oí cáscaras sobre el nuevo proyecto, nada confirmado.
Translation: I only heard rumors about the new project, nothing confirmed.

Oye, men
A casual way to address someone, similar to "hey, man."
Example: Oye, men, ¿qué haces aquí?
Translation: Hey, man, what are you doing here?

Onda
A vibe or trend.
Example: Esa es la onda del momento, todos están hablando de eso.
Translation: That's the current trend; everyone is talking about it.

Ojo de tigre
A keen or sharp look.
Example: Necesito que me des tu ojo de tigre para resolver este problema.
Translation: I need your sharp eye to solve this problem.

Oscuro
A term for something secretive or shady.
Example: Hay algo oscuro en ese negocio, no me gusta.
Translation: There's something shady about that deal; I don't like it.

Odiar a muerte
To strongly dislike or hate.
Example: Odio a muerte ese tipo de comida.
Translation: I strongly dislike that type of food.

Ojo con eso
Be careful with that.
Example: Ojo con eso, podría romperse fácilmente.
Translation: Be careful with that; it could break easily.

Oír campanas y no saber dónde
To hear something and not fully understand it.
Example: Estás oyendo campanas y no sabes dónde, infórmate bien.
Translation: You're hearing something and don't understand it; get properly informed.

Ojo de sapo
A nickname for someone who is overly observant.
Example: No te pongas tan ojo de sapo, no es para tanto.
Translation: Don't be so observant; it's not that serious.

Ojo del huracán
The calm center of a chaotic situation.
Example: En medio del caos, él fue el ojo del huracán, mantuvo la calma.
Translation: In the midst of chaos, he was the calm center, keeping composure.

Ojo avizor
A vigilant or watchful eye.

Example: Debes tener un ojo avizor con los detalles del proyecto.
Translation: You need to be vigilant with the project details.

Ojo de cristal
A term for someone who is overly sensitive.
Example: No te pongas con ojo de cristal por cualquier comentario.
Translation: Don't be overly sensitive to every comment.

Ojo de lince
A sharp eye, someone who notices everything.
Example: Ella tiene un ojo de lince para detectar errores.
Translation: She has a sharp eye for spotting mistakes.

P

Panameño
A person from Panama.
Example: Soy panameño, nací y crecí aquí.
Translation: I'm Panamanian; I was born and raised here.

Pana
Friend or buddy.
Example: Ese es mi pana; lo conozco desde hace años.
Translation: That's my buddy; I've known him for years.

Pato
A term for someone who is cheap or stingy.
Example: No seas pato, paga tu parte de la cuenta.
Translation: Don't be cheap; pay your share of the bill.

Pillar
To catch or find something.
Example: Me pilla si ves algo interesante.
Translation: Let me know if you find something interesting.

Pindín
A term for someone who is stingy or cheap.
Example: Ese tipo es un pindín, nunca gasta en nada.
Translation: That guy is cheap; he never spends on anything.

Pelu
A term for someone who is stylish or fashionable.
Example: Esa chica siempre está pelu con su ropa.
Translation: That girl is always stylish with her clothes.

Pito
A term for a whistle or something that's not serious.
Example: No le prestes atención, es solo un pito.
Translation: Don't pay attention; it's just nonsense.

Peliar con el mueble
To be stuck in a difficult or boring situation.
Example: Estoy peliando con el mueble en esta reunión interminable.
Translation: I'm stuck in this never-ending meeting.

Papaleta
A fool or silly person.
Example: No seas papaleta, no te tomes las cosas tan en serio.
Translation: Don't be silly; don't take things so seriously.

Pita
A term for something trivial or insignificant.
Example: Eso no es más que una pita, no vale la pena.
Translation: That's just trivial; it's not worth it.

Pola
Beer.
Example: Vamos por unas polas después del trabajo.
Translation: Let's go for some beers after work.

Pijo
Someone who is posh or pretentious.
Example: Ella se cree muy pijo con sus ropas caras.
Translation: She thinks she's very posh with her expensive clothes.

Pelao
A young person or child.
Example: Ese pelao tiene mucho talento.
Translation: That kid has a lot of talent.

Pasarla bien
To have a good time.
Example: La pasamos bien en la fiesta anoche.
Translation: We had a good time at the party last night.

Pata de perro
Someone who is always out and about.
Example: Mi amigo es una pata de perro, siempre está viajando.
Translation: My friend is always out and about; he's always traveling.

Pase de lista
Attendance or checking who's present.
Example: El profesor hace el pase de lista al principio de cada clase.
Translation: The teacher takes attendance at the beginning of each class.

Pintar cara
To show anger or disappointment.
Example: Pintó cara cuando vio el resultado.
Translation: He showed his disappointment when he saw the result.

Pico de oro
A smooth talker or someone who is very persuasive.

Example: Con su pico de oro, siempre logra convencer a la gente.
Translation: With his smooth talk, he always manages to persuade people.

Punto
A detail or key point.
Example: No olvides este punto en tu presentación.
Translation: Don't forget this key point in your presentation.

Q

Que chuzo
Expression of surprise or admiration.
Example: ¡Que chuzo, nunca lo había visto antes!
Translation: How cool, I've never seen that before!

Que bola
Expression of disbelief or amazement.
Example: ¡Que bola! No puedo creer que pasó esto.
Translation: Wow! I can't believe this happened.

Que vaina
A term for a problem or hassle.
Example: ¡Que vaina, se me olvidaron los documentos!
Translation: What a hassle, I forgot the documents!

Que pereza
Feeling of laziness or boredom.
Example: ¡Que pereza, no tengo ganas de hacer nada hoy!
Translation: What a drag; I don't feel like doing anything today!

Que nivel
Expression to describe something or someone of high quality or excellence.
Example: ¡Que nivel, tu presentación fue excelente!
Translation: What a level; your presentation was excellent!

Que locura
Expression for something crazy or unbelievable.
Example: ¡Que locura, no puedo creer lo que pasó!
Translation: How crazy; I can't believe what happened!

Que rollo
A term for a complicated situation or problem.
Example: Ese proyecto es un que rollo, nunca se acaba.
Translation: That project is a hassle; it never ends.

Que pena
Expression of sympathy or embarrassment.
Example: ¡Que pena que no pude asistir a tu fiesta!
Translation: I'm sorry I couldn't attend your party!

Que estufa
A term for someone who is very attractive or hot.
Example: Esa chica es una que estufa, todos la miran.
Translation: That girl is very attractive; everyone is looking at her.

Que bien
Expression of approval or satisfaction.
Example: ¡Que bien, ya terminaste el proyecto!
Translation: That's great; you finished the project!

Que guapo
Compliment for someone who looks handsome or attractive.
Example: ¡Qué guapo te ves hoy!
Translation: You look handsome today!

Que tal
Casual greeting or inquiry about how someone is doing.
Example: ¡Hola, qué tal! ¿Cómo te va?
Translation: Hi, how's it going?

Que cool
Expression of approval or admiration.
Example: ¡Qué cool, me encanta tu nueva chaqueta!
Translation: How cool; I love your new jacket!

Que chamba
A term for a tough job or hard work.
Example: Eso es una que chamba, pero vale la pena.
Translation: That's a tough job, but it's worth it.

Que gusto
Expression of pleasure or satisfaction.
Example: ¡Qué gusto verte de nuevo!
Translation: It's a pleasure to see you again!

Que duro
Expression of admiration for something impressive or tough.
Example: ¡Qué duro está ese juego, no puedo ganarlo!
Translation: How tough that game is; I can't win it!

Que flaca
A term for someone who is very thin.
Example: Mira qué flaca está desde que empezó a hacer ejercicio.
Translation: Look how thin she's gotten since she started exercising.

Que chido
Expression of excitement or approval.
Example: ¡Qué chido tu nuevo coche!
Translation: How cool your new car is!

Que pasa
Casual way to ask what's happening.
Example: ¡Hola, qué pasa! ¿Todo bien?
Translation: Hi, what's up? All good?

Que liada
A term for a complicated or messy situation.
Example: ¡Qué liada, no sé cómo resolver esto!
Translation: What a mess; I don't know how to solve this!

R

Rolo
A term for someone from Bogotá (Colombian) used to describe someone as sophisticated.
Example: Ese tipo es un rolo, siempre está vestido a la moda.
Translation: That guy is sophisticated; he's always dressed fashionably.

Rumba
A party or celebration.
Example: Vamos a la rumba esta noche.
Translation: Let's go to the party tonight.

Rico
Delicious or someone who is attractive.
Example: Esa comida está rica, ¡me encanta!
Translation: This food is delicious; I love it!

Rata
A term for someone who is cheap or stingy.
Example: Ese es un rata, siempre busca evitar gastar dinero.
Translation: He's stingy; he always looks for ways to avoid spending money.

Rápido como un rayo
Very fast.
Example: Corre rápido como un rayo, siempre llega primero.
Translation: He runs as fast as lightning; he always arrives first.

Rata de dos patas
A derogatory term for someone deceitful or untrustworthy.
Example: No confíes en él; es una rata de dos patas.
Translation: Don't trust him; he's untrustworthy.

Rollo
A term for a story or situation.
Example: Te voy a contar el rollo completo de lo que pasó.
Translation: I'll tell you the whole story of what happened.

Rico en matices
Something rich in details or nuances.
Example: Su presentación fue rica en matices, muy completa.
Translation: His presentation was rich in details, very thorough.

Rumbear
To go out partying or clubbing.
Example: Este fin de semana vamos a rumbear en la discoteca.
Translation: This weekend we're going out clubbing.

Rata de biblioteca
A bookworm or someone who reads a lot.
Example: Mi hermano es una rata de biblioteca, siempre está leyendo.
Translation: My brother is a bookworm; he's always reading.

Reventar

To break or burst.
Example: La fiesta estaba tan llena que casi revienta.
Translation: The party was so packed that it almost burst.

Raspado
Barely passing or failing a test.
Example: Solo pasé el examen raspado; necesito estudiar más.
Translation: I barely passed the exam; I need to study more.

Ronda
A round or a series of drinks.
Example: Vamos a pedir otra ronda de cervezas.
Translation: Let's order another round of beers.

S

Salsa
A lively dance genre or a lively event.
Example: Vamos a la salsa, que hay una fiesta increíble.
Translation: Let's go to the party; there's an amazing event.

Sapo
A snitch or someone who reveals secrets.
Example: No le digas nada; es un sapo.
Translation: Don't tell him anything; he's a snitch.

Súper
An expression for something that is excellent or outstanding.
Example: La película estuvo súper; la recomendaría a todos.
Translation: The movie was excellent; I would recommend it to everyone.

Sapo verde
A term for someone who is overly inquisitive.
Example: No seas sapo verde, no es asunto tuyo.
Translation: Don't be overly inquisitive; it's none of your business.

Seguir la corriente
To go along with something or follow the trend.
Example: A veces es mejor seguir la corriente para evitar problemas.
Translation: Sometimes it's better to go along with things to avoid problems.

Soltar
To release or let go.
Example: Suelta el estrés y disfruta del momento.
Translation: Let go of the stress and enjoy the moment.

Súbito
Sudden or abrupt.
Example: Hubo un cambio súbito en el clima.
Translation: There was a sudden change in the weather.

Sapo de otro pozo
Someone who is out of place or doesn't belong.
Example: Se siente como un sapo de otro pozo en esa reunión.
Translation: He feels out of place in that meeting.

Saco
A term for someone who is very bad at something.
Example: Eres un saco para jugar al fútbol.
Translation: You're really bad at playing soccer.

Sabrás qué hacer
Expression meaning you'll know what to do.
Example: No te preocupes, sabrás qué hacer en el momento.
Translation: Don't worry, you'll know what to do when the time comes.

Saber a poco
To feel insufficient or unsatisfying.
Example: La cena estuvo buena, pero me supo a poco.

Translation: The dinner was good, but it felt insufficient.

Sombra de un recuerdo
A faint memory or reminiscence.
Example: El lugar es solo la sombra de un recuerdo.
Translation: The place is just a shadow of a memory.

T

Tico
A term for someone from Costa Rica.
Example: Soy tico, y con mucho orgullo.
Translation: I'm Costa Rican, and I'm very proud of it.

Tumbao
A term for someone with style or rhythm.
Example: Tiene un tumbao único en la pista de baile.
Translation: He has a unique style on the dance floor.

Tostón
A slang term for something boring or tiresome.
Example: La reunión fue un tostón; no se habló de nada interesante.
Translation: The meeting was boring; nothing interesting was discussed.

Tico
A term for someone from Costa Rica.
Example: Soy tico, y con mucho orgullo.
Translation: I'm Costa Rican, and I'm very proud of it.

Tumbao
A term for someone with style or rhythm.
Example: Tiene un tumbao único en la pista de baile.
Translation: He has a unique style on the dance floor.

Tostón
A slang term for something boring or tiresome.
Example: La reunión fue un tostón; no se habló de nada interesante.

Translation: The meeting was boring; nothing interesting was discussed.

Temor
Fear or apprehension.
Example: Siento un gran temor antes de dar una presentación.
Translation: I feel great apprehension before giving a presentation.

Tetero
A term for a baby bottle.
Example: El bebé necesita su tetero antes de dormir.
Translation: The baby needs his bottle before sleeping.

Tetero
A term for a baby bottle.
Example: El bebé necesita su tetero antes de dormir.
Translation: The baby needs his bottle before sleeping.

Tóxico
A term for something or someone harmful or unpleasant.
Example: Ese ambiente es tóxico, mejor alejarse.
Translation: That environment is toxic; better stay away.

U

Uña y carne
A term for very close friends or inseparable people.
Example: Ellos son uña y carne; siempre están juntos.
Translation: They are inseparable; they are always together.

Unas
Some or a few.
Example: Necesito unas horas para terminar el trabajo.
Translation: I need a few hours to finish the work.

Último
Last or final.
Example: Es el último capítulo del libro, ¡está emocionante!
Translation: It's the last chapter of the book; it's exciting!

Una vez
Once or one time.
Example: Solo lo he visto una vez en mi vida.
Translation: I've only seen him once in my life.

Ultimátum
An ultimatum or final demand.
Example: El jefe nos dio un ultimátum para entregar el proyecto.
Translation: The boss gave us an ultimatum to deliver the project.

Usual

Usual or customary.
Example: Es mi rutina usual levantarse temprano.
Translation: It's my usual routine to wake up early.

Utopia
An ideal or perfect place or state.
Example: Su idea de una utopía es un mundo sin conflictos.
Translation: His idea of a utopia is a world without conflicts.

Unido
United or close-knit.
Example: La familia está muy unida y siempre se apoya.
Translation: The family is very united and always supports each other.

V

Vacilón
A fun or lively event.
Example: La fiesta fue un vacilón; todos se divirtieron mucho.
Translation: The party was a blast; everyone had a great time.

Venga
Come on or let's go.
Example: ¡Venga, no llegaremos tarde!
Translation: Come on, we'll be late!

W

Wari
A slang term for someone who is very cool or impressive.
Example: Ese tipo es un wari, siempre sabe cómo impresionar.
Translation: That guy is cool; he always knows how to impress.

Wapa
A term for a hit or something that is a success.
Example: La nueva canción es un wapa, está en todas partes.
Translation: The new song is a hit; it's everywhere.

Wiri
A term for something that is exciting or interesting.
Example: La película tiene un wiri que te mantendrá al borde del asiento.
Translation: The movie has excitement that will keep you on the edge of your seat.

Whas
A term used to ask what's going on.
Example: ¿Whas, cómo estás hoy?
Translation: What's up, how are you today?

Wacky
A term for something or someone that is very eccentric or strange.
Example: Esa fiesta estuvo wacky, con todas las decoraciones locas.

Translation: That party was wacky, with all the crazy decorations.

Wairo
A term for a tough or strong person.
Example: Ese tipo es un wairo; no se deja intimidar por nada.
Translation: That guy is tough; he doesn't get intimidated by anything.

Wit
A term for someone who is witty or clever.
Example: Tienes un wit muy agudo; siempre me haces reír.
Translation: You have a sharp wit; you always make me laugh.

Wisa
A slang term for something that is very cool or impressive.
Example: Esa moto es wisa, me encantaría tener una igual.
Translation: That bike is cool; I'd love to have one like it.

Wara
A term used to describe a wild or energetic person.
Example: Ella es una wara, siempre está llena de energía.
Translation: She's wild; she's always full of energy.

Worm
A term for someone who is sneaky or deceptive.
Example: No confíes en él; es un worm que siempre está buscando problemas.
Translation: Don't trust him; he's sneaky and always looking for trouble.

Wepa
An expression used to show enthusiasm or approval.
Example: ¡Wepa, lo lograste!
Translation: Awesome, you did it!

Waka
A term for a good or impressive performance.
Example: El cantante hizo un waka durante el concierto.
Translation: The singer gave an impressive performance during the concert.

Made in United States
North Haven, CT
12 July 2025